Pueblo Indians
of the Southwest

By Mira Bartók and
Christine Ronan

GoodYearBooks

An Imprint of ScottForesman
A Division of HarperCollinsPublishers

United States

The Pueblo Indians live in
the southwestern states of
New Mexico and Arizona.

Pueblo means "town" in Spanish.
Long ago, the Pueblo Indians' ancestors
built towns into the sides of mountains.

Sometimes they made pictures
on cliff walls and rocks.

5

6

Today, some Pueblo Indians live
in pueblos on high, flat mountains
called *mesas*.

There is very little rain
where they live. Rain is
important to farmers
who need water to raise
corn and other crops
for food.

Some say that a rain cloud
is a gift of life from the
ancestor spirits.

People thank these spirits in many ways—
with ceremonies, dancing, drumming,
and by making beautiful objects.

Some call the ancestor spirits that bring rain during the growing season *kachinas*.

These dolls are models of kachinas.

The dolls help children to remember
the many kachina spirits.

Elders teach the ways of their ancestors, keeping ancient traditions alive.